THE CHINESE HOROSCOPES LIBRARY

RABBIT

KWOK MAN-HO

A DORLING KINDERSLEY BOOK

Senior Editor   Sharon Lucas
Art Editor   Camilla Fox
Managing Editor   Krystyna Mayer
Managing Art Editor   Derek Coombes
DTP Designer   Doug Miller
Production Controller   Antony Heller
US Editor   Laaren Brown

Artworks: Danuta Mayer 4, 8, 11, 17, 27, 29, 31, 33, 35;
Giuliano Fornari 21; Jane Thomson; Sarah Ponder.

Special Photography by Steve Gorton. Thank you to The British Museum, Chinese Post
Office, Percival David Foundation of Chinese Art, and The Powell-Cotton Museum.

Additional Photography: Eric Crichton, Jo Foord, Steve Gorton, Dave King, Martin Norris,
Tim Ridley.

Picture Credits: Circa Photo Library 12, 18; Percival David Foundation of Chinese Art 23bl,
Royal Geographical Society 25tr.

First American Edition, 1994
4 6 8 10 9 7 5 3

Published in the United States by DK Publishing, Inc., 95 Madison Avenue,
New York, New York 10016

Visit us on the World Wide Web at
http://www.dk.com

ISBN 1-56458-606-5
Library of Congress Catalog Number 93-48006

Reproduced by GRB Editrice, Verona, Italy
Printed and bound in Hong Kong by Imago

CONTENTS

INTRODUCING CHINESE HOROSCOPES

For thousands of years, the Chinese have used their astrology and religion to establish a harmony between people and the world around them.

The exact origins of the twelve animals of Chinese astrology – the Rat, Ox, Tiger, Rabbit, Dragon, Snake, Horse, Ram, Monkey, Rooster, Dog, and Pig – remain a mystery. Nevertheless, these animals are important in Chinese astrology. They are much more than general signposts to the year and to the possible good or bad times ahead for us all. The twelve animals of Chinese astrology are considered to be a reflection of the Universe itself.

YIN AND YANG
The many differences in our natures, moods, health, and fortunes reflect the wider changes within the Universe. The Chinese believe that

YIN AND YANG SYMBOL
White represents the female force of yin, and black represents the masculine force of yang.

every single thing in the Universe is held in balance by the dynamic, cosmic forces of yin and yang. Yin is feminine, watery, and cool; the force of the Moon and the rain. Yang is masculine, solid, and hot; the force of the Sun and the Earth. According to ancient Chinese belief, the concentrated essences of yin and yang became the four seasons, and the scattered essences of yin and yang became the myriad creatures that are found on Earth.

The twelve animals of Chinese astrology are all associated with either yin or yang. The forces of yin rise as Winter approaches. These forces decline with the warmth of Spring, when yang begins to assert itself. Even in the course of a normal day, yin and yang are at work, constantly changing and balancing. These forces also naturally rise and fall within us all.

Everyone has their own internal balance of yin and yang. This affects our tempers, ambitions, and health. We also respond to the changes of weather, to the environment, and to the people who surround us.

THE FIVE ELEMENTS

All that we can touch, taste, or see is divided into five basic types or elements – wood, fire, earth, gold, and water. Everything in the Universe can be linked to one of these elements.

For example, the element wood is linked to the Tiger and to the Rabbit. This element is also linked to the color green, sour-tasting food, the season of Spring, and the

emotion of anger. The activity of these elements indicates the fortune that may befall us.

AN INDIVIDUAL DISCOVERY

Chinese astrology can help you balance your yin and yang. It can also tell you which element you are, and the colors, tastes, parts of the body, or emotions that are linked to your particular sign. Your fortune can be prophesied according to the year, month, day, and hour in which you were born. You can identify the type of people to whom you are attracted, and the career that will suit your character. You can understand your changes of mood, your reactions to other places and to other people. In essence, you can start to discover what makes you an individual.

DIVINATION STICKS
Another ancient and popular method of Chinese fortune-telling is using special divination sticks to obtain a specific reading from prediction books.

CASTING YOUR HOROSCOPE

The Chinese calendar is based on the movement of the Moon, unlike the calendar used in the Western world, which is based on the movement of the Sun.

Before you begin to cast your Chinese horoscope, check your year of birth on the chart on pages 44 to 45. Check particularly carefully if you were born in the early months of the year. The Chinese year does not usually begin until January or February, and you might belong to the previous Chinese year. For example, if you were born in 1961 you might assume that you were born in the Year of the Ox. However, if your birthday falls before February 15 you belong to the previous Chinese year, which is the Year of the Rat.

THE SIXTY-YEAR CYCLE

The Chinese measure the passing of time by cycles of sixty years. The twelve astrological animals appear five times during the sixty-year cycle, and they appear in a slightly different form every time. For example, if you were born in 1951

you are a Rabbit in the Burrow, but if you were born in 1963, you are a Rabbit Running in the Forest.

MONTHS, DAYS, AND HOURS

The twelve lunar months of the Chinese calendar do not correspond exactly with the twelve Western calendar months. This is because Chinese months are lunar, whereas Western months are solar. Chinese months are normally twenty-nine to thirty days long, and every three to four years an extra month is added to keep approximately in step with the Western year.

One Chinese hour is equal to two Western hours, and the twelve Chinese hours correspond to the twelve animal signs.

The year, month, day, and hour of birth are the keys to Chinese astrology. Once you know them, you can start to unlock your personal Chinese horoscope.

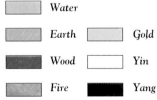

Water

Earth   Gold

Wood   Yin

Fire   Yang

CHINESE ASTROLOGICAL WHEEL
*In the center of the wheel is the yin and
yang symbol. It is surrounded by the
Chinese astrological character linked to
each animal. The band of color indicates
your element, and the outer ring reveals
whether you are yin or yang.*

· RABBIT ·
MYTHS AND LEGENDS

*The Jade Emperor, heaven's ruler, asked to see the Earth's twelve
most interesting animals. When they arrived, he was impressed
by the Rabbit's sleekness, and awarded it fourth place.*

The Rabbit is a symbol of longevity and is believed to live in the Moon, where it slowly grinds the Pill of Immortality with a mortar and pestle. There is an ancient Chinese belief that only female rabbits exist. They were thought to become

pregnant by eating plant shoots and to give birth by spitting their young from their mouths.

BUDDHA AND THE RABBIT

Long ago, the Buddha came to a remote forest. He had traveled for many days, and was tired and hungry. The animals of the forest were all determined to serve him in the best possible way. They gathered together and decided to find food for him. Each animal brought the food that it naturally harvested.

The rabbit thought of bringing some grass. "I like grass," thought the rabbit, "so I expect the Buddha will, too." So he found a patch of fresh

THE MOON GODDESS

The gods carried Princess Sheung Ngao to the Moon to escape her violent husband. She lives there with the Rabbit, shown on the bottom left of this Chinese tablet.

RABBIT MIRROR

This bronze mirror shows the Rabbit using a mortar and pestle to grind the Pill of Immortality. It derives from the Sung dynasty (960–1279).

green grass and started to eat it. When the whole patch was gone, the rabbit suddenly realized what he had done. Next he found some succulent leaves to bring to the Buddha. "After all," said the rabbit, "I like leaves, so I expect the Buddha will, too." He started to eat, and soon there was not a leaf in sight.

Crestfallen, the rabbit brought himself before the Buddha. "O Buddha," said the rabbit, "I am a foolish creature and have nothing to give you except myself. Please eat me if you are hungry." The Buddha was touched by the rabbit's willingness to give up his own life. He placed his hand on the rabbit, and the rabbit flew up to the Moon.

Here, the Buddha set him down, and explained that he would be seen for the rest of time by those on the Earth looking at the Moon.

The Buddha had given the Rabbit the supreme gift of eternal life. Even today, if you look at the Moon, you will see the Rabbit, forever grinding the Pill of Immortality.

· RABBIT ·
PERSONALITY

The Rabbit has a tranquil and generous character, and a youthful and imaginative outlook. It is sensitive and is happiest when it is in harmony with its environment.

Your moods are easily affected by people, objects, or the environment in which you find yourself. You can only relax once you have checked everything out to your satisfaction.

MOTIVATION
While most people are spurred into action by exciting opportunities and challenges, you tend to hold yourself back until you are absolutely sure what lies ahead. Conflict and aggression make you nervous. You much prefer to remain in the background rather than seizing the limelight. It is only when you are cornered that you attack – if there is the remotest possibility of an escape route, you will take it immediately.

THE INNER RABBIT
You are happiest when the troubles of your everyday life are behind you and when you feel secure. However, sometimes security can be a little too safe, and there is a possibility that you will miss out on very

PORCELAIN RABBIT
The fine brushstrokes and natural coloring on this Chinese porcelain rabbit give it an astonishingly lifelike appearance.

JUMPING RABBITS

This highly colored porcelain plate depicts five rabbits in Autumn. Four rabbits are jumping around the outer rim, and one rabbit is feeding in the center. The plate dates from the Ch'ing dynasty of 19th-century China.

positive opportunities. Your overriding need for security can make you obstinate. Luckily, when your friends need help you are always there, as long as your moral principles are not remotely compromised.

Your warmth and hospitality are enhanced by your excellent sense of refinement, and when you feel at ease in groups you are charming, elegant, and well informed.

Hospitality is one of your natural talents – you are rarely happier than when you are at home entertaining your friends. You are faithful, agreeable, and easygoing. In emotional relationships you are a loving partner, but your tenderness must be returned. You are equally loving and caring in a parental role, but you are not always confident about the best way to cope with the domestic and emotional upheavals of everyday family life.

THE RABBIT CHILD

The young Rabbit is pleasant, obedient, and hardworking. It is often bashful and reticent, and will need plenty of love and encouragement to develop its confidence.

· RABBIT ·
LOVE

The Rabbit loves to be loved and needs to be treated with care. It is easily upset by erratic passions and is happiest when it is sustaining a peaceful relationship.

When you find yourself attracted to someone, you are not afraid to show your kindness and affection, for this is your way of winning the object of your desires. If your tenderness is returned, both you and the relationship will blossom, but if you do not receive constant, loving care, the relationship will fade.

You are sensitive, and if you find yourself in an emotional conflict that cannot be resolved, your health is likely to suffer. In the search for a committed relationship you may appear to be fickle, but you are simply testing various relationships until you are sure that

you have found the right partner. Once you have found a soulmate, you are devoted and find the mere thought of parting virtually unbearable.

Ideally, you are suited to the Pig or the Ram. You share a love of peace, solitude, and honesty with the Pig, but it might prove too outrageous for your conservative nature. The creative and imaginative Ram also wants a peaceful

GODDESS OF LOVE
Kuan Yin is a powerful figure in Chinese mythology. Once a male Buddhist deity, she is now known as the goddess of mercy, and as Sung-tzu, the giver of children.

CHINESE COMPATIBILITY WHEEL

Find your animal sign, then look for the animals that share its background color – the Rabbit has a green background and is most compatible with the Ram and the Pig. The symbol in the center of the wheel represents double happiness.

life, and you should bring a sense of security and seriousness to the relationship.

The Monkey's wily ways and good advice will be greatly enjoyed by you, and the Monkey will appreciate your discretion and sympathetic nature. The warmth and passion of the Horse could attract you, and you can offer it your ample resources of comfort and love. The Snake shares your love of peace

ORCHID

In China, the orchid, or Lan Hua, is an emblem of love and beauty. It is also a fertility symbol and represents many offspring.

and beauty, and you will be able to teach it tolerance. The Dog seeks security, and you should find its protective, honest nature appealing.

The Rat's excessive emotions are likely to disturb your precious tranquillity, but a relationship with another Rabbit is likely to be too quiet and peaceful for both of you. The energy of the charismatic Dragon could be irritating, and you may find that your patience is easily exhausted by the excitable and exhibitionistic Rooster.

· RABBIT ·
CAREER

The Rabbit has a professional, honest, and meticulous approach to work, but it is not personally ambitious. It is happiest if it can work in a harmonious environment.

RABBIT SAUCER
The Rabbit's attitude to its career is just as modest and gentle as the Rabbit depicted on this Chinese saucer. The saucer is decorated with blue underglaze and originates from the Wanli period of the Ming dynasty (1573–1620).

Chinese porcelain saucer

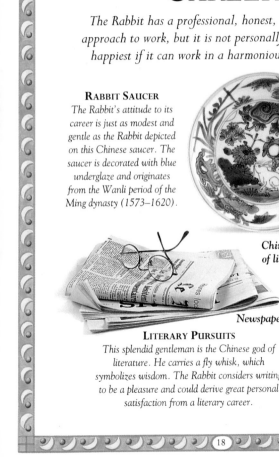

Chinese god of literature

Newspapers

LITERARY PURSUITS
This splendid gentleman is the Chinese god of literature. He carries a fly whisk, which symbolizes wisdom. The Rabbit considers writing to be a pleasure and could derive great personal satisfaction from a literary career.

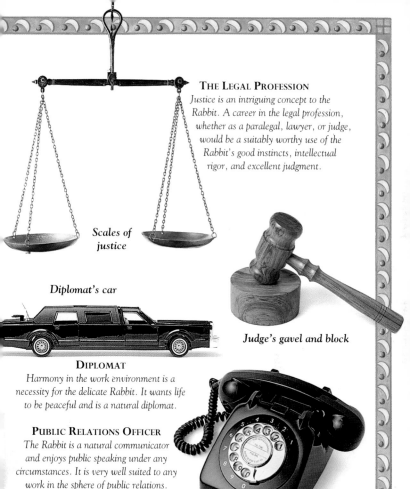

THE LEGAL PROFESSION
Justice is an intriguing concept to the Rabbit. A career in the legal profession, whether as a paralegal, lawyer, or judge, would be a suitably worthy use of the Rabbit's good instincts, intellectual rigor, and excellent judgment.

Scales of justice

Diplomat's car

Judge's gavel and block

DIPLOMAT
Harmony in the work environment is a necessity for the delicate Rabbit. It wants life to be peaceful and is a natural diplomat.

PUBLIC RELATIONS OFFICER
The Rabbit is a natural communicator and enjoys public speaking under any circumstances. It is very well suited to any work in the sphere of public relations.

Bakelite telephone

HEALTH

Yin and yang are in a continual state of flux within the body. Good health is dependent upon the balance of yin and yang being constantly harmonious.

There is a natural minimum and maximum level of yin and yang in the human body. The body's energy is known as ch'i and is a yang force. The movement of ch'i in the human body is complemented by the movement of blood, which is a yin force. The very slightest displacement of the balance of yin or yang in the body can lead to poor health. Yang illness can be cured by yin treatment, and yin illness can

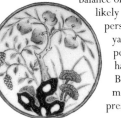

LINGCHIH FUNGUS

The fungus shown in this detail from a Ch'ing dynasty bowl is the "immortal" lingchih fungus, which symbolizes longevity.

be cured by yang treatment. Everybody has their own individual balance of yin and yang. It is likely that a hot-tempered person will have strong yang forces, and that a peaceful person will have strong yin forces. Before Chinese medicine can be prescribed, your moods have to be carefully taken into account. A balance of joy, anger, sadness, happiness, worry, pensiveness, and fear must be maintained. This fine balance is known as the Harmony of the Seven Sentiments.

CARDAMOM

This aromatic, pleasant-tasting East Indian fruit is related to the ginger family.

Born in the Year of the Rabbit, you are associated with the element wood. This element is linked with the liver, gallbladder, tendons, and eyes. These are the parts of the human body that are most relevant to the pattern of your health. You are also associated with the emotion of anger and with sour-tasting food.

The fruit cardamom (*Elettaria cardamomum*) is associated with your Chinese astrological sign. It is often ground and used as a flavoring, and its seeds can be used as a spice. Cardamom is both yin and yang, and is consequently prescribed for its warming and cooling properties. It is reputed to be a restorer of balance and can renew the body's vitality. It is also used to calm nausea and to prevent vomiting.

The use of Chinese medicine is highly specific; therefore, never take cardamom or any other medicinal herb unless you are following professional advice from a fully qualified Chinese or Western doctor.

ASTROLOGY AND ANATOMY

Your element, wood, is particularly associated with the liver and the gall-bladder. The liver is a yin organ, and the gallbladder is a yang organ.

LEISURE

The Rabbit is a friendly, sociable creature. It enjoys taking part in many activities, but tends to avoid any pastimes that involve an element of risk.

Cricket ball, bails, stumps, and bat

TABLE TENNIS
As long as other people organize and direct an activity, such as table tennis, the Rabbit is more than happy to join in.

Early table-tennis, or Ping-Pong, equipment

CRICKET
The Rabbit is fairly conservative and enjoys traditional – even obscure – sports, such as cricket.

Elegant shoes

DRESSING UP

The Rabbit is renowned for its excellent dress sense and will seize any opportunity to express it. Dinner parties or intimate gatherings with friends are a double source of pleasure for the Rabbit – not only can it dress up in its favorite clothes, but it can also enjoy the company of others.

Material swatches

Chinese rabbit figurine

INTERIOR DESIGN

Comfort and good taste are all that the Rabbit demands in its home life, and it likes to create a classic home environment.

Soft cushion

RESTING RABBIT

This exquisite Chinese figurine of a resting rabbit dates from the T'ang dynasty (618–906).

SYMBOLISM

*Each astrological animal is linked with a certain food,
direction, color, emotion, association, and symbol. The
Rabbit is also associated with the season of Spring.*

**Chinese fitting
with rabbits**

COLOR

*In China, green is the color of Spring, happiness, and
inner peace. Green is also the color that is associated
with the Rabbit. This verdigris bronze Chinese fitting is
from the Chou dynasty (c. 1100BC–901BC).*

FOOD

*There are five tastes according to
Chinese astrology – salty, acrid,
bitter, sour, and sweet. Sour
foods, such as cranberries, are
linked with the Rabbit.*

Cranberries

Antique Chinese compass

David Livingstone's compass

DIRECTION
The Chinese compass points south, whereas the Western compass points north. The Rabbit's direction is the east.

SYMBOL
The Rabbit's symbol in Chinese astrology is the compass.

ASSOCIATION
The field of agriculture is linked with the Rabbit.

EMOTION
Anger is the emotion that is connected with the Rabbit.

Angry baby

Cereal crops

BUDDHA RABBIT

~ 1915 1975 ~

*In Chinese mythology, there are many Rabbits who gave
their lives for Buddhist saints and deities. Reputedly, the
Buddha was a Rabbit in a previous life.*

In the West, the Rabbit tends to be considered a fluffy, slightly weak animal, and it is a favorite children's pet. In China, however, the Rabbit enjoys considerable status and is highly regarded. It is perceived as being a particularly strong and determined animal.

THE RABBIT AND THE BUDDHA

There are many powerful links between the Rabbit and the Buddha in Chinese belief, and consequently, those born in the year of the Buddha Rabbit should consider themselves fortunate. You are likely to be a highly skilled individual, well organized, and always prepared for the unexpected.

PERSONALITY

You are associated with fulfillment and have a powerful, auspicious personality. You invariably know exactly what you want from life and deliberately set out to achieve your goals. Your determination should serve you well, and you are always likely to achieve the majority of your goals in life.

All Buddha Rabbits are highly likely to be stubborn. This can be both an asset and a problem. If you can control this tendency to be difficult, you should find that life is considerably more enjoyable, both for you and for other people.

FEMALE CHARACTERISTICS

Because of the calming effects of the yin influence, the female Buddha Rabbit can expect to enjoy a long, fulfilled life.

She is likely to be a leader or pioneer, and probably possesses immense energy. This energy should carry her to success, as well as ensuring her longevity.

Buddha Rabbit

CAREER

The goals and desires of Buddha Rabbits are not necessarily selfish. Like the Buddha himself, you are often philanthropic. Instead of seeking personal power, wealth, and success in your career, you try to direct your innate skills and forcefulness toward those who are less fortunate than yourself.

You tend to be more than willing to fight for causes that are close to your heart and will risk being unpopular to achieve your aims. Your intelligence and powers will invariably help you succeed.

Other people are often highly impressed by your principled stand or sheer determination against the odds. Often people in positions of authority will offer you help, and this should never be refused.

FRIENDSHIPS

Given the opportunity, you tend to always make the best of any situation. However, when exploiting your opportunities, try to ensure that this is not at other people's expense. If you allow yourself to go too far, you could eventually lose your friends' love and respect.

RABBIT LOOKING AT THE MOON

~ 1927 1987 ~

The Moon is an auspicious sign to have as a Rabbit. When the Chinese look at the full moon, they see a Rabbit grinding the Pill of Immortality.

You are associated with strength of character and endurance. People tend to trust you implicitly and to look up to you. Using all your skills, you do your job thoroughly.

PERSONALITY

You are equally at ease with either the intellectual or the technical, and do not shine in any one field. Instead, you tend to be gifted in many ways and are valued for your willingness to become a part of whatever is happening around you.

You take immense pride in your appearance and are blessed with excellent dress sense. This love of appearances extends to the places in which you live and work. You need an attractive working environment, and your home must be a place where everyone feels relaxed and aesthetically pleased.

FEMALE CHARACTERISTICS

The female Rabbit Looking at the Moon can sometimes be accused of being temperamental. There is an element of truth in this accusation, but if she manages to balance her skills with her frustration, her generous nature should dominate.

Nevertheless, she should make every effort to curb her tendency toward excessive complaining or grumbling. She is always likely to be respected for her skills, for they are considerable, but she may be resented and will probably be considered irritating if she stirs up too much trouble.

CAREER

Work is never a problem for Rabbits born in these years. They are skillful and versatile, and should always be in considerable demand.

Rabbit Looking at the Moon

FRIENDSHIPS
You are linked with the nail, symbolizing that you are the pivot to much of what goes on around you. Like most Rabbits, you invariably inspire good friendships.

RELATIONSHIPS
In emotional matters, any Rabbit Looking at the Moon should make a very good partner for the right person. This is because you have very high standards and are enjoyable company. You are usually well balanced, do not take offense easily, and have a forgiving nature.

Do try to watch out for the odd flash of temper, however, because it can be damaging, not least because it is so unexpected. As long as you are always quick to apologize, all should eventually turn out well.

Rabbit Running Out of the Forest

~ 1939 1999 ~

The Rabbit Running Out of the Forest is a nervous creature.
It rarely wishes to emphasize its individuality and is
happiest in the security of a large group.

You are associated with the interweaving of a thread through cloth. Symbolically, this means that you always want to be part of what is going on around you and to have a clear place within it.

Personality

You are sometimes considered to be a curious Rabbit – nervous and easily startled by anything out of the ordinary. Your highly developed sense of alarm makes you anxious and prone to worry. All Rabbits loathe disagreement and argument, but you tend to dislike them even more than most.

You are prone to worry if you find yourself pulled out of context or standing out above the rest. You are happiest when you are part of the flow of life and can quietly pursue your own interests.

Education

Throughout your life it is likely that you will be successful, but not to any outstanding extent. At school, your teachers probably recognized that you were a good student, but were essentially part of the crowd.

Career

Your career may follow a similar pattern – you never want to be perceived as an individualistic standout. However, it is possible that you will rise to high positions because of your natural willingness to be an integral part of a team, company, or group.

It is unlikely that you will attain a highly exalted position, however, because this goes against your wish to be part of the general flow of life. You will have increased authority and wealth, though, if you can

Rabbit Running Out of the Forest

continue to operate as part of a team and manage not to panic when you experience difficulties.

RELATIONSHIPS

In emotional matters, it would perhaps be better for you to choose a partner who is older than you. An older partner will help to reassure you and to make you feel more secure and loved.

Because you do not take unnecessary risks and do not relish the strain of doing things alone, it is likely that you will have a long, fulfilled life and a happy committed relationship. You are likely to have a full social life, and your innate friendliness and enjoyment of beautiful things will ensure that others will always feel comfortable and relaxed around you.

FAMILY

Do not be surprised if you have problems with your parents, since they may sometimes find it very difficult to understand you. As long as you stay calm, however, they should be able to treat you as an adult, and you will all enjoy a fulfilling relationship.

RABBIT IN THE BURROW

~ 1951 2011 ~

*According to appearances, this is a perfectly happy Rabbit
— comfortable and secure in its natural habitat. The
burrow, however, can also represent confinement.*

You are often anxious and insecure, even when you may seem to have few problems. You find it hard to accept what you have at the present moment and are anxious about what the future might bring.

When you should be feeling relaxed and happy, you frequently find yourself caught up with trivial anxieties. You probably feel this way because you are associated with causing offense and the resulting punishment. Try to relax and enjoy the security of being a Rabbit in the Burrow instead.

PERSONALITY
Your inner tensions can sometimes make you seem rather blunt — you find it hard to be polite. You give your truthful, honest opinion when asked. This trait can often be a virtue, but if it gets mixed up with your personal anxieties, then it can

become aggressive. Try to control this characteristic and take a little time to think before you speak.

If you distinguish between what is worth saying and what comes to your mind, you are likely to gain a valuable reputation for wisdom.

RELATIONSHIPS
You should have a good committed relationship with your partner, but you must learn to control yourself and develop your self-confidence.

You have the potential to sustain a long relationship, even though both you and your partner may have to honestly face any fears and worries that lurk below the surface.

FAMILY
At first, your family is likely to disapprove of your choice of partner, but do not worry unduly. You should find that if you are patient and

Rabbit in the Burrow

give them enough time to make up their own minds, then they are more likely to accept, and like, your choice. Try not to hurry them, for they will invariably come around to your way of thinking.

PROSPECTS
Once you have managed to curb the acerbic side of your personality successfully, and have healthily processed your inner tensions, you should find that your life becomes immensely rich and rewarding.

You tend to be strongly independent, and whether you are at school, work, or leisure, people in positions of authority are likely to always further your interests and offer you their support. As you get older, this support should bring you increasing good fortune.

RABBIT RUNNING IN THE FOREST

~ 1903 1963 ~

The Rabbit Running in the Forest has a good life. It is safe from predators and can find plenty of food and shelter. This points to a very successful personality.

The Chinese believe in ancestor worship – that is, if their ancestors are not given due respect, then they can make life difficult for their unruly descendants.

The Rabbit Running in the Forest is particularly associated with ancestor worship. This means that, at times, if you fail to be thoughtful and considerate, life can be difficult – your behavior is upsetting your dead ancestors, and they are making you suffer as a result.

Luckily, this association can also have a positive influence – if you think of others as well as yourself, then the benefits of such worthy actions are considerable.

PERSONALITY
You have the potential for success and happiness in work, leisure, and family relationships. This is largely dependent upon how you deal with others, however. Always try to remember other people, in particular those who are less fortunate than you and those who could wield some influence over your life.

Because you can often turn difficulty into success, you can sometimes seem unsympathetic to those who find life harder. If you try to develop your charitable instincts, you should find that you become a much better person, and other people will enjoy being around you even more.

YOUTH
Invariably, it takes some time for you to realize the need to balance your own sense of confidence with some thought for others. In your youth, you are likely to find that you do not do quite as well as you expect.

Rabbit Running in the Forest

Undoubtedly you have the potential for success, but somehow it keeps being frustrated.

Be patient, and do not give in to feelings of despair. By learning to consider other people, and by listening to the wisdom of those in authority, you will find that advancement and success will invariably be achieved as you mature.

CAREER
People in authority can have a truly beneficial impact both on your career and on your life. Remember always to be dutiful and respectful, even though you may sometimes feel that the world is your oyster.

RELATIONSHIPS
This is also true in regard to your personal relationships. You are likely to be an extremely attractive and attentive person, but you sometimes need to beware of occasional feelings of complacency and self-satisfaction. Once you have found the right partner, however, you should be able to enjoy a very long and happy committed relationship.

YOUR CHINESE MONTH OF BIRTH

Find the table with your year of birth, and see where your birthday falls. For example, if you were born on August 30, 1951, you were born in Chinese month 7.

1   You are clever and calm. You inspire friendship and respect, but shun fame and lavish fortune.

2   You are naturally cautious. Try to take risks in order to make the most of your opportunities.

3   You are single-minded, but should not ignore the potential richness of a more varied life.

4   You tend to overvalue yourself, and to despise less successful people. Learn to accept criticism.

5   You are morally courageous and decisive. These qualities allow you to be at peace with yourself.

6   You combine enthusiasm with pragmatism, and optimism with realism. Success should be yours.

7   You are sensible and popular, but too cautious. Learn to follow your sense of intuition instead.

8   You tend to be too hasty when you make decisions, but can easily change misfortune to good fortune.

9   You may seem uncaring, but your feelings are deep. Express yourself in order to achieve success.

10   You are spontaneous, generous, and have a tendency to make dramatic gestures. Try to relax.

11   You are caring, and a good judge of character. Your wisdom should ensure a successful future.

12   You are complex – outwardly calm, but in turmoil within. Learn to control your inner forces.

* Some Chinese years contain double months:	
1903: Month 5	1963: Month 4
May 27 – June 24	April 24 – May 22
June 25 – July 23	May 23 – June 20
1987: Month 6	
June 26 – July 25	
July 26 – Aug 23	

1903	
Jan 29 – Feb 26	1
Feb 27 – March 28	2
March 29 – April 26	3
April 27 – May 26	4
See double months box	5
July 24 – Aug 22	6
Aug 23 – Sept 20	7
Sept 21 – Oct 19	8
Oct 20 – Nov 18	9
Nov 19 – Dec 18	10
Dec 19 – Jan 16 1904	11
Jan 17 – Feb 15	12

1915	
Feb 14 – March 15	1
March 16 – April 13	2
April 14 – May 13	3
May 14 – June 12	4
June 13 – July 11	5
July 12 – Aug 10	6
Aug 11 – Sept 8	7
Sept 9 – Oct 8	8
Oct 9 – Nov 6	9
Nov 7 – Dec 6	10
Dec 7 – Jan 4 1916	11
Jan 5 – Feb 2	12

1927	
Feb 2 – March 3	1
March 4 – April 1	2
April 2 – April 30	3
May 1 – May 30	4
May 31 – June 28	5
June 29 – July 28	6
July 29 – Aug 26	7
Aug 27 – Sept 25	8
Sept 26 – Oct 24	9
Oct 25 – Nov 24	10
Nov 24 – Dec 23	11
Dec 24 – Jan 22 1928	12

1939	
Feb 19 – March 20	1
March 21 – April 19	2
April 20 – May 18	3
May 19 – June 16	4
June 17 – July 16	5
July 17 – Aug 14	6
Aug 15 – Sept 12	7
Sept 13 – Oct 12	8
Oct 13 – Nov 10	9
Nov 11 – Dec 10	10
Dec 11 – Jan 8 1940	11
Jan 9 – Feb 7	12

1951	
Feb 6 – March 7	1
March 8 – April 5	2
April 6 – May 5	3
May 6 – June 4	4
June 5 – July 3	5
July 4 – Aug 2	6
Aug 3 – Aug 31	7
Sept 1 – Oct 30	8
Oct 1 – Oct 29	9
Oct 30 – Nov 28	10
Nov 29 – Dec 27	11
Dec 28 – Jan 26 1952	12

1963	
Jan 25 – Feb 23	1
Feb 24 – March 24	2
March 25 – April 23	3
See double months box	4
June 21 – July 20	5
July21 – Aug 18	6
Aug 19 – Sept 17	7
Sept 18 – Oct 16	8
Oct 17 – Nov 15	9
Nov 16 – Dec 15	10
Dec 16 – Jan 14 1964	11
Jan 15 – Feb 12	12

1975	
Feb 11 – March 12	1
March 13 – April 11	2
April 12 – May 10	3
May 11 – June 9	4
June 10 – July 8	5
July 9 – Aug 6	6
Aug 7 – Sept 5	7
Sept 6 – Oct 4	8
Oct 5 – Nov2	9
Nov 3 – Dec 2	10
Dec 3 – Dec 31	11
Jan 1 – Jan 30 1976	12

1987	
Jan 29 – Feb 27	1
Feb 28 – March 28	2
March 29 – April 27	3
April 28 – May 26	4
May 27 – June 25	5
See double months box	6
Aug 24 – Sept 22	7
Sept 23 – Oct 22	8
Oct 23 – Nov 20	9
Nov 21 – Dec 20	10
Dec 21 – Jan 18 1988	11
Jan 19 – Feb 16	12

1999	
Feb 16 – March 17	1
March 18 – April 15	2
April 16 – May 14	3
May 15 – June 13	4
June 14 – July 12	5
July 13 – Aug 10	6
Aug 11 – Sept 9	7
Sept 10 – Oct 8	8
Oct 9 – Nov 7	9
Nov 8 – Dec 7	10
Dec 8 – Jan 6 2000	11
Jan 7 – Feb 4	12

YOUR CHINESE DAY OF BIRTH

Refer to the previous page to discover the beginning of your Chinese month of birth, then use the chart below to calculate your Chinese day of birth.

If you were born on May 5, 1903, your birthday is in the month starting on April 27. Find 27 on the chart below. Using 27 as the first day, count the days until you reach the date of your birthday. (Remember that not all months contain 31 days.) You were born on day 9 of the Chinese month.

If you were born in a Chinese double month, simply count the days from the first date of the month that contains your birthday.

1	2	3	4	5	6	7
8	9	10	11	12	13	14
15	16	17	18	19	20	21
22	23	24	25	26	27	28
29	30	31				

DAY 1, 10, 19, OR 28

You are trustworthy and set high standards, but tend to rush your projects. Try to be cautious, and do not be too self-obsessed. You may receive unexpected money but must control your spending. You are suited to a career in the public sector or the arts.

DAY 2, 11, 20, OR 29

You are honest and popular. You need peace, but also require lively company. You are prone to outbursts of temper. You tend to enjoy life and make the most of your opportunities. You are suited to a literary or artistic career.

DAY 3, 12, 21, OR 30

You are quick-witted, but may appear to be difficult. As a result, people may be wary of being your friend. You have a disciplined character and fight for the truth. You are suited to careers that have a competitive element.

Day 4, 13, 22, or 31

You are very warmhearted, but also have a reserved attitude, which can sometimes make you appear unapproachable. If you try to be more outgoing and sociable, you should become more popular. You have a calm and patient manner, and are suited to a career as an academic or researcher.

Day 5, 14, or 23

Your fiery, obstinate nature can sometimes make it difficult for you to accept suggestions or opinions from others, and your stubbornness may lead to quarrels or problems. You should be lucky with money and may often use your profits to set up new projects. Your innate intelligence will enable you to cope with a demanding career.

Day 6, 15, or 24

You have an open, stable, and cheerful character, and enjoy an active social life. You are affectionate and emotional, and have a tendency to daydream. This can lead to confusion, and your eagerness to help others may be stifled by your indecision. Although you will never be wealthy, you should always have enough money.

Day 7, 16, or 25

You enjoy a certain amount of excitement in your life, but must learn to become more realistic and disciplined. Although you are a natural performer, you should beware of alienating your friends or colleagues. In your career, the opportunity to travel is more important to you than a good salary or a high standard of living.

Day 8, 17, or 26

You have very good judgment, but should not act too quickly. Your social skills may sometimes be lacking, and you may alienate other people, so try to be more tactful. You will experience poverty, but also wealth. Your calm and determined nature is combined with a free spirit, making you best suited to self-employment.

Day 9, 18, or 27

You are happy, optimistic, and warmhearted. You keep yourself busy and are rarely troubled by trivialities. Occasionally you quarrel unnecessarily with your friends, and it is important for you to learn to control your moods. You are particularly suited to a career as a sole owner or proprietor.

YOUR CHINESE
HOUR OF BIRTH

*In Chinese time, one hour is equal to two Western hours.
Each Chinese double hour is associated with one of the
twelve astrological animals.*

11 P.M. – 1 A.M. RAT HOUR
You are independent and have a hot temper. Try to think before you speak. Your thrifty nature will be useful in business and at home. You are willing to help those who are close to you, and they will return your support.

1 – 3 A.M. OX HOUR
Up to the age of twenty, your life could be difficult, but your fortunes are likely to improve after these troublesome years. In your career, be prepared to take a risk or to leave home during your youth to achieve your goals. You should enjoy a prosperous old age.

3 – 5 A.M. TIGER HOUR
You have a lively and creative nature, which may cause family arguments in your youth. Between the ages of twenty and forty you may have many problems. Luckily, your fortunes are likely to improve dramatically in your forties.

5 – 7 A.M. RABBIT HOUR
Your parents should be helpful, but your siblings may be your rivals. You may have to move away from home to achieve your full potential at work. Your committed relationship may take time to become settled, but you should get along much better with everyone after middle age.

7 – 9 A.M. DRAGON HOUR
You have a quick-witted, determined, and attractive nature. Your life will be busy, but you could sometimes be lonely. You should achieve a good standard of living. Try to curb your excessive self-confidence, for it could make working relationships difficult.

9 – 11 A.M. SNAKE HOUR

You have a talent for business and should find it easy to build your career and provide for your family. You have a very generous spirit and will gladly help your friends when they are in trouble. Unfortunately, family relationships are unlikely to run smoothly.

11 A.M. – 1 P.M. HORSE HOUR

You are active, clever, and obstinate. Try to listen to advice. You are fascinated with travel and with changing your life. Learn to control your extravagance, for it could lead to financial suffering.

1 – 3 P.M. RAM HOUR

Steady relationships with your family, friends, or partners are difficult, because you have an active nature. You are clever, but must not force your views on others. Your fortunes will be at their lowest in your middle age.

3 – 5 P.M. MONKEY HOUR

You earn and spend money easily. Your character is attractive, but frustrating, too. Sometimes your parents are not able to give you adequate moral support. Your committed relationship should be good, but do not brood over emotional problems for too long – if you do your career could suffer.

5 – 7 P.M. ROOSTER HOUR

In your teenage years you may have many arguments with your family. There could even be a family division, which should eventually be resolved. You are trustworthy, kind, and warmhearted, and never intend to hurt other people.

7 – 9 P.M. DOG HOUR

Your brave, capable, hard-working nature is ideally suited to self-employment, and the forecast for your career is excellent. Try to control your impatience and vanity. The quality of your life is far more important to you than the amount of money you have saved.

9 – 11 P.M. PIG HOUR

You are particularly skilled at manual work and always set yourself high standards. Although you are warmhearted, you do not like to surround yourself with too many friends. However, the people who are close to you have your complete trust. You can be easily upset by others, but are able to forgive and forget quickly.

YOUR FORTUNE IN OTHER ANIMAL YEARS

The Rabbit's fortunes fluctuate during the twelve animal years. It is best to concentrate on a year's positive aspects, and to take care when faced with the seemingly negative.

 YEAR OF THE RAT
Minor and irritating problems can occur, but the Year of the Rat is generally a good year for the Rabbit. Try to stay calm at all times, and remember that this year there is nothing that you cannot cope with as long as you continue to persevere.

 YEAR OF THE OX
This is likely to be a difficult year, and you could find yourself confronted with a variety of pressing problems. Take adequate care of yourself at all times, and learn to spend more time looking after your physical and mental health.

 YEAR OF THE TIGER
Distress is likely to affect you from all quarters in the Year of the Tiger. Do not give in to despair, however. As long as you keep a relatively low, uncontroversial profile, you should remain unscathed.

 YEAR OF THE RABBIT
As you might expect, the Year of the Rabbit is an exceptionally good year for the Rabbit. You should find that everything you decide to try your hand at will run extremely smoothly and successfully, and you could even become quite famous.

 YEAR OF THE DRAGON
After the successful excesses of last year, it is important that you remain firmly in touch with reality in the Year of the Dragon. Do not set unrealistic targets for yourself this year, because they will invariably end in disappointment.

YEAR OF THE SNAKE

Your professional life is likely to take you away from your home this year. Although this will undoubtedly offer you many new and exciting opportunities to grow, it will also inevitably place stress and strain on your family life.

YEAR OF THE HORSE

Good fortune is yours throughout the Year of the Horse, and you will spend a considerable portion of the year enjoying celebrations and other social events. Make the most of this splendid time, because it is unlikely to last forever.

YEAR OF THE RAM

This is a year in which you feel unsettled in various areas of your life, and it will be most beneficial if you try to keep your own counsel. Do not be rash this year – watch events carefully, then decide on the correct course of action.

YEAR OF THE MONKEY

Although the start of the Year of the Monkey is likely to be poor and disappointing, you should not lose heart. As long as you remain calm, sensible, and patient, your position in life is bound to improve by the end of the year.

YEAR OF THE ROOSTER

You will need a considerable store of energy in the Year of the Rooster. You are likely to be subjected to exhausting hardship this year and are prone to legal arguments and even disasters.

YEAR OF THE DOG

Although the Year of the Dog will start with good fortune, you should by no means take it for granted. Always try to make the very most of your success this year, and do not allow petty disagreements and disputes to disrupt and spoil it.

YEAR OF THE PIG

Problems and illnesses are likely to stalk you throughout the Year of the Pig, but luckily, they should only be minor. Although you may find them irritating, they should not prevent you from enjoying a fairly good year.

YOUR CHINESE
YEAR OF BIRTH

*Your astrological animal corresponds to the Chinese year of
your birth. It is the single most important key in the quest
to unlock your Chinese horoscope.*

Find your Western year of birth in
the left-hand column of the chart.
Your Chinese astrological animal is
on the same line as your year of birth
in the right-hand column of the
chart. If you were born in the
beginning of the year, check the

middle column of the chart carefully.
For example, if you were born in
1964, you might assume that you
belong to the Year of the Dragon.
However, if your birthday falls
before February 13, you actually
belong to the Year of the Rabbit.

1900	Jan 31 – Feb 18, 1901	Rat
1901	Feb 19 – Feb 7, 1902	Ox
1902	Feb 8 – Jan 28, 1903	Tiger
1903	Jan 29 – Feb 15, 1904	Rabbit
1904	Feb 16 – Feb 3, 1905	Dragon
1905	Feb 4 – Jan 24, 1906	Snake
1906	Jan 25 – Feb 12, 1907	Horse
1907	Feb 13 – Feb 1, 1908	Ram
1908	Feb 2 – Jan 21, 1909	Monkey
1909	Jan 22 – Feb 9, 1910	Rooster
1910	Feb 10 – Jan 29, 1911	Dog
1911	Jan 30 – Feb 17, 1912	Pig
1912	Feb 18 – Feb 5, 1913	Rat
1913	Feb 6 – Jan 25, 1914	Ox
1914	Jan 26 – Feb 13, 1915	Tiger
1915	Feb 14 – Feb 2, 1916	Rabbit
1916	Feb 3 – Jan 22, 1917	Dragon

1917	Jan 23 – Feb 10, 1918	Snake
1918	Feb 11 – Jan 31, 1919	Horse
1919	Feb 1 – Feb 19, 1920	Ram
1920	Feb 20 – Feb 7, 1921	Monkey
1921	Feb 8 – Jan 27, 1922	Rooster
1922	Jan 28 – Feb 15, 1923	Dog
1923	Feb 16 – Feb 4, 1924	Pig
1924	Feb 5 – Jan 23, 1925	Rat
1925	Jan 24 – Feb 12, 1926	Ox
1926	Feb 13 – Feb 1, 1927	Tiger
1927	Feb 2 – Jan 22, 1928	Rabbit
1928	Jan 23 – Feb 9, 1929	Dragon
1929	Feb 10 – Jan 29, 1930	Snake
1930	Jan 30 – Feb 16, 1931	Horse
1931	Feb 17 – Feb 5, 1932	Ram
1932	Feb 6 – Jan 25, 1933	Monkey
1933	Jan 26 – Feb 13, 1934	Rooster

1934	Feb 14 – Feb 3, 1935	Dog
1935	Feb 4 – Jan 23, 1936	Pig
1936	Jan 24 – Feb 10, 1937	Rat
1937	Feb 11 – Jan 30, 1938	Ox
1938	Jan 31 – Feb 18, 1939	Tiger
1939	Feb 19 – Feb 7, 1940	Rabbit
1940	Feb 8 – Jan 26, 1941	Dragon
1941	Jan 27 – Feb 14, 1942	Snake
1942	Feb 15 – Feb 4, 1943	Horse
1943	Feb 5 – Jan 24, 1944	Ram
1944	Jan 25 – Feb 12, 1945	Monkey
1945	Feb 13 – Feb 1, 1946	Rooster
1946	Feb 2 – Jan 21, 1947	Dog
1947	Jan 22 – Feb 9, 1948	Pig
1948	Feb 10 – Jan 28, 1949	Rat
1949	Jan 29 – Feb 16, 1950	Ox
1950	Feb 17 – Feb 5, 1951	Tiger
1951	Feb 6 – Jan 26, 1952	Rabbit
1952	Jan 27 – Feb 13, 1953	Dragon
1953	Feb 14 – Feb 2, 1954	Snake
1954	Feb 3 – Jan 23, 1955	Horse
1955	Jan 24 – Feb 11, 1956	Ram
1956	Feb 12 – Jan 30, 1957	Monkey
1957	Jan 31 – Feb 17, 1958	Rooster
1958	Feb 18 – Feb 7, 1959	Dog
1959	Feb 8 – Jan 27, 1960	Pig
1960	Jan 28 – Feb 14, 1961	Rat
1961	Feb 15 – Feb 4, 1962	Ox
1962	Feb 5 – Jan 24, 1963	Tiger
1963	Jan 25 – Feb 12, 1964	Rabbit
1964	Feb 13 – Feb 1, 1965	Dragon
1965	Feb 2 – Jan 20, 1966	Snake
1966	Jan 21 – Feb 8, 1967	Horse
1967	Feb 9 – Jan 29, 1968	Ram
1968	Jan 30 – Feb 16, 1969	Monkey
1969	Feb 17 – Feb 5, 1970	Rooster
1970	Feb 6 – Jan 26, 1971	Dog

1971	Jan 27 – Feb 14, 1972	Pig
1972	Feb 15 – Feb 2, 1973	Rat
1973	Feb 3 – Jan 22, 1974	Ox
1974	Jan 23 – Feb 10, 1975	Tiger
1975	Feb 11 – Jan 30, 1976	Rabbit
1976	Jan 31 – Feb 17, 1977	Dragon
1977	Feb 18 – Feb 6, 1978	Snake
1978	Feb 7 – Jan 27, 1979	Horse
1979	Jan 28 – Feb 15, 1980	Ram
1980	Feb 16 – Feb 4, 1981	Monkey
1981	Feb 5 – Jan 24, 1982	Rooster
1982	Jan 25 – Feb 12, 1983	Dog
1983	Feb 13 – Feb 1, 1984	Pig
1984	Feb 2 – Feb 19, 1985	Rat
1985	Feb 20 – Feb 8, 1986	Ox
1986	Feb 9 – Jan 28, 1987	Tiger
1987	Jan 29 – Feb 16, 1988	Rabbit
1988	Feb 17 – Feb 5, 1989	Dragon
1989	Feb 6 – Jan 26, 1990	Snake
1990	Jan 27 – Feb 14, 1991	Horse
1991	Feb 15 – Feb 3, 1992	Ram
1992	Feb 4 – Jan 22, 1993	Monkey
1993	Jan 23 – Feb 9, 1994	Rooster
1994	Feb 10 – Jan 30, 1995	Dog
1995	Jan 31 – Feb 18, 1996	Pig
1996	Feb 19 – Feb 6, 1997	Rat
1997	Feb 7 – Jan 27, 1998	Ox
1998	Jan 28 – Feb 15, 1999	Tiger
1999	Feb 16 – Feb 4, 2000	Rabbit
2000	Feb 5 – Jan 23, 2001	Dragon
2001	Jan 24 – Feb 11, 2002	Snake
2002	Feb 12 – Jan 31, 2003	Horse
2003	Feb 1 – Jan 21, 2004	Ram
2004	Jan 22 – Feb 8, 2005	Monkey
2005	Feb 9 – Jan 28, 2006	Rooster
2006	Jan 29 – Feb 17, 2007	Dog
2007	Feb 18 – Feb 6, 2008	Pig